Birthing Praise

OUT OF

Your Pain

30 DAYS DEVOTIONAL

BIRTHING PRAISE

OUT OF YOUR PAIN

---

30 Days Devotional

Desrene Stewart

PUBLISHING HOUSE. A Division of
Business Startup and Marketing
Solutions LLC

ISBN: 978-1736801529

Books are available at quantity discounts with bulk purchase for educational, businesses, or sales promotional use. Please email mdmtransform@gmail.com or desrenes@live.com for further information, to place book orders or to book Pastor Desrene Stewart for speaking opportunity offers.

Introduction

Genesis 29:17 talks about a woman by the name of Leah. She was described as having "delicate or weak eyes". Much was not said about her. But can you imagine how having this description could have made her feel. This verse became real to me when I experienced one of what I called the worst periods of my life. It was during this period that I believed the Lord planted a seed in me that developed into one of the most important messages I ever shared. God had to allow me to go through this experience because of what he was getting ready to birth out of me. For this to take place, I had to be still enough to have an intimate moment with the Holy Spirit for the conception of what he wanted to grow in me to take place.

Conception is a process; it cannot take place in the natural or in the spirit unless you have a moment of intimacy with God or another person. This moment may include the Holy Spirit helping you to understand who you are in Christ and what His plans are for you. Knowing who you are is critical because if you do not, you will not have the proper insight as to what you can birth out. Don't be afraid to become one with the Holy Spirit. He is waiting to have a moment with you. He has great plans and wants to help you fulfill them all.

WHO AM I?

"For I know the plans I have for you," declares the Lord, "plans to prosper you and not to harm you, plans to give you hope and a future" (Jer. 29:11, NIV).

Who am I? is such a loaded question. Many times, we are not even sure how to answer when we are asked. Did I always believe Jeremiah 29:11? Did I know that God really had a plan for my life? Did I know that the process He was taking me through to bring me into greatness was not meant to kill me? Absolutely not! This verse became real to me when I experienced one of the most painful processes in my life. During this time frame I wrestled with God because I did not understand why I was in the position that I was in. Have you ever been there? That place of wrestling with God because you wanted an answer and the one you were getting was not the one you wanted to hear? I remember being introduced to a great woman of God who asked me, "Do you know who you are?" When I was asked that question, I was a bit perplexed and answered, "I am a woman of God". She looked at me with much love and said, "The day you understand who you are, you will do great exploits for God".

To fully understand Jeremiah 29:11, I had to understand Psalms 139:14-16 where the writer praises God when he understands how much time God put into framing and creating him. There had to be an understanding of how much time God put into creating me and that I am fearfully and wonderfully made regardless of how others see me. I had to understand that inside me was a butterfly waiting to be born. If I did not understand who I was and am becoming, I would have never made it through the transition of emerging into that butterfly.

Do you know who you are? Do you know that God created you with greatness and no one can take that away from you? Do you know you are a son or a daughter of the King? Do you know you are deeply loved by Christ, and you don't have to do anything to earn it? Do you know you have been blessed in heavenly places with every spiritual blessing? Do you know you are precious in the sight of God, and he called you the "apple of His eyes"? Understanding who you are holds the key to becoming who God destined you to become. As we journey together, I know God will unfold His great plans for you as you transition into what He is calling you to.

Prayer - Father I thank you for fearfully and wonderfully creating me in your image. I thank you Father that even though I may not have a full understanding of who I am, you are working in and through me to reveal that and for others to see. Holy Spirit when I forget who I am, please remind me through your Word. Remind me that your plans for me are to give me hope and a great future. I thank you for your assurance of love and guidance. I think that as I grow to know you more, you will reveal more of who you are and more of who I am becoming. In Jesus' name, amen.

Reflection

Who Am I?

"For I know the plans I have for you," declares the Lord, "plans to prosper you and not to harm you, plans to give you hope and a future"- (Jer. 29:11 NIV).

What is God telling me today?

____

____

____

____

____

____

____

What am I praying for today?

____

____

____

____

____

____

____

____

A Heart of Gratitude

Be thankful in all circumstances, for this is God's will for you who belong to Christ Jesus." - 1 Thessalonians 5:18 (NLT)"

Today I am thankful for:

DON'T BE DEFINED BY OTHERS

16 "Now Laban had two daughters; the name of the older was Leah, and the name of the younger was Rachel." 17 "Leah had weak[a] eyes, but Rachel had a lovely figure and was beautiful."–Genesis 29:16-17 (NIV)

Leah's eyes were described as weak! Some translations used the word "delicate". When I read the story of Leah — which my Birthing Praise message was born out of — I was saddened because of how the writer described her. Of all the attributes she possessed, this was the one that was written about her. Can you imagine how this must have made her feel? Can you imagine how low her self-esteem must have been? Can you imagine how inferior she must have felt to her sister Rachel? Do you allow others to define you by your attributes or by how they feel about you? Being defined by others can be demeaning because it allows others to say how they see you and what they believe you are. Don't ever let your self-worth be tied to someone else's. Some people will try to define you by your past mistakes. Being here means that your past did not destroy or deter you. Sometimes those mistakes we make in our past help to

Strengthen our future. Don't allow others to make you feel inadequate because God has already placed everything in you that you need to succeed. The kind of life that we live depends on how we see ourselves. God has already declared that you are fearfully and wonderfully made according to Psalms 139. When God created you, He knew exactly what He was doing. He did not make a mistake. He created you in His image and likeness and you are the epitome of who He is. Never allow others to dress you in their apparel. You were never created to be defined by anyone but the Father Himself. He created you! He has the final say-so in how you are defined because when you were formed in your mother's womb, he already defined who you were before you were brought forth in the earth realm. Your definition comes from the Father. Walk into who and what He has defined you to be. No one can make you feel inferior without your consent!

Prayer – Father I thank you that I am a son/daughter of the King. I thank you for crowning me with righteousness and making me to be heirs and joint heirs with you. I thank you for creating me in your image and likeness and your DNA runs through me because I am your child. Holy Spirit remind me that nothing I say or do will separate me from your great love and I am not condemned because I am in you. I thank you that I am walking in heavenly places and despite my flaws and imperfection, you still love me. In Jesus' name, amen.

Reflection

<u>Don't Be Defined by Other</u>

"Now Laban had two daughters; the name of the older was Leah, and the name of the younger was Rachel. 17 Leah had weak[a] eyes but Rachel had a lovely figure and was beautiful." (Gen. 29:16-17, NIV)

What is God telling me today?

____

____

____

____

____

____

____

What am I praying for today?

____

____

____

____

____

____

____

____

A Heart of Gratitude

Therefore, since we are receiving a kingdom which cannot be shaken, let us have grace, by which we may serve God acceptably with reverence and godly fear. For our God is a consuming fire."

- Hebrews 12:28-29 (NKJV)

Today I am thankful for:

FEELING UNLOVED

"Jacob made love to Rachel also, and his love for Rachel was greater than his love for Leah." (Gen. 29:30, NIV)

Have you ever felt unloved? Felt like no one loved you because you did not look like them, act like them and in some cases weren't as pretty/handsome as they were? Welcome to Leah's world! She became a part of a puzzle that she did not quite fit into. It would not have been her choice. Her father made the choice for her, and she had to live with the consequence of being unloved.

Sometimes we define love based on the experiences we have had and unless we experience the true love of Christ, we will never know what true love is. When we want to know the true meaning of the word love, we just need to look at John 3:16. This verse is the epitome of what true love represents. God demonstrated his love in such a tangible way that he gave His only begotten son. It is hard for someone to love when they have never experienced true love. Jacob experienced so much turmoil in his family that he did not quite understand the true meaning of love.

When we feel unloved, it is not from God. It's the enemy's way of

letting us believe that no one loves us. Once we have accepted Christ as our personal Savior, we get to experience a love like no other; true love that can only come from God. Sometimes we are trying to find love in the wrong places and through the wrong medium. You don't have to go looking for love, the love of God will find you! Feeling unloved will affect many other areas of your life and cause you to question who you are. The bible is filled with scriptures that tell us how much God loves us. Engulf yourself in a few (John 3:16; John 4:8; John 4:9-11; 1 John 4:16; Isaiah 54:10; Romans 5:8; Psalms 136:26) and feel Christ's loving arms being wrapped around you.

Prayer – Father, there are times that I don't feel loved. There are times when I question even the love that you have for me. Help me to remember that your Son made the ultimate sacrifice so that I can experience true love. I will experience true love because your Word tells me that your love for me is unfailing. I take comfort in knowing that nothing can and will separate me from your love. In Jesus' name, amen.

Reflection

Feeling Unloved

"Jacob made love to Rachel also, and his love for Rachel was greater than his love for Leah." (Gen. 29:30, NIV)

What is God telling me today?

What am I praying for today?

A Heart of Gratitude

"I thank you for answering my prayer and giving me victory!" -Psalm 118:21(NLT)

Today I am thankful for:

HE SEES YOUR PAIN

"When the Lord saw that Leah was not loved, he enabled her to conceive, but Rachel remained childless."- (Gen. 29:31, NIV)

Tears are a language that God understands. Sometimes when we are going through pain, we feel as if God is not seeing, and no one understands. Leah felt this way. God fully understood what Leah was going through and He was getting ready to let her know that he felt her pain and was about to begin blessing her. God knows where you are! He sees what is going on in your life and the bible tells us that He is touched with the feelings of our infirmities. He has not forgotten about you. He has not left you alone. He has not abandoned you when it seems like you need Him the most. The bible tells us to wait on the Lord and be of good courage and He shall strengthen our hearts. It is hard when someone is going through a season where everything is going wrong to tell them to be of good courage. But it does not matter what the situation looks like on the outside, God is working it out for our good.

Pain has its good and bad points. Pain is what our body uses to let us know that something is wrong. Sometimes God uses our pain to bring uneasiness in our current state so He can launch us into our destiny. Joseph's pain of being in the pit, brought him to the palace. The servant girl's pain of being captured allowed her master Naaman to experience his healing. Your pain can become your passport into your future. Being in pain and not feeling loved can cause us to go into isolation and not want fellowship with others. The enemy wants to use our pain to keep us in isolation, so we are separated from those we know love us and to let us believe that no one cares. God assured Leah that He not only saw her pain, but He was getting ready to do something about the pain she was feeling. It is important to understand during your time of pain that God sees you.

If you feel like God is not seeing what you are going through, rest assured that He does. Pour your heart out to Him and begin to shift your focus from the pain and allow the Holy Spirit to minister to your heart. He does care! Psalms 61:2 tells us that when our heart is overwhelmed, we can go to the rock that is higher than we are to find comfort. If you are burdened down, Matthew 11:28-29 tells us that we can take his yoke and find rest in Him.

Prayer – Father I am thankful that tears are a language that you understand. When I am feeling overwhelmed from my pain and struggles, I can come to you and find rest. Help me not to lean on my own understanding, but in all my ways, learn to acknowledge you so that you can direct my path as I go through my season of pain. Help me, Holy Spirit not to be anxious about anything, but to bring all my requests to you so that your peace can guard my heart and mind. In Jesus' name, amen.

He Sees Your Pain

"When the Lord saw that Leah was not loved, he enabled her to conceive, but Rachel remained childless."- (Gen. 29:31, NIV)

What is God telling me today?

What am I praying for today?

A Heart of Gratitude

"For the Lord is the great God, the great King above all gods."

Psalm 95:3 (NIV)

Today I am thankful for:

OPEN WOMB

"When the LORD saw that Leah was unloved,

He opened her womb; but Rachel was barren."-

(Gen. 29:31, KJV)

When the Lord saw that Leah was hated, he opened her womb (Gen. 29:31 KJV). For God to open Leah's womb, it must have been shut. The womb is such an important part of a woman's body. It is the place where conception takes place and protection is given. One of the Hebrew words that is translated as the word womb in scripture is the word "rechem". It is the word for compassion and mercy. The root meaning is "protection from harm". The womb is a place of protection for babies. It is said to be the safest place for babies to be protected from harm.

When Mary went to see Elizabeth — not knowing she was pregnant — the bible said that the baby (John, the Baptist) leaped in her womb. God will place people in your life when He opens your womb, to be witnesses to what you are carrying and cause what you are carrying to move. God wants to protect us and what we are carrying; He allows us to be locked up in the womb of the spirit so what we are carrying can be protected until we get to our next destination.

When God opens our womb and opens doors in our lives and anything else that has been shut up, no man can shut it back. I pray that as you read these words, God is opening your womb and positioning you to conceive. I believe that whatever has been shut up, is getting ready to open up. Just as the walls of Jericho came tumbling down, all your shut doors and fortified walls are getting ready to come down in the Name of Jesus!

Sometimes we go through situations where we feel barren or empty. Your womb was not closed because you are barren, God had to shut up your womb because what you were carrying was too important and it had to be protected. Your womb must be open so you can conceive, closed to prevent miscarriage, but open so you can deliver. God shut up Hannah's womb in 1 Samuel 1:6 because it was not yet the season for Samuel the Prophet to come forth. God will keep your womb closed until the season for your conception to take place. Wait on the Lord. He has the right timing when He will open your womb to birth out what has been placed within it.

Prayer – Father I thank you for the ability to conceive. I thank you that when my womb was closed I was not barren, but you were trying to protect what you placed in it. I pray that the seed that you placed in my womb will come forth during the right season. I pray I will bring forth in the right season what you placed in me. Give me the strength to carry what has been placed in me. I thank you for opening doors that no man can shut and shutting doors that no man can open. In Jesus' name, amen.

Reflection

Open Womb

"When the LORD saw that Leah was unloved, He opened her womb; but Rachel was barren." (Gen. 29:31, KJV)

What is God telling me today?

What am I praying for today?

A Heart of Gratitude

"Rejoice always, pray continually, give thanks in all circumstances; for this is God's will for you in Christ Jesus." _1 Thessalonians 5:16-18(NIV)

Today I am thankful for:

INTIMACY WITH GOD

"Come close to God, and God will come close to you. Wash your hands, you sinners; purify your hearts, for your loyalty is divided between God and the world." (James 4:8, NLT)

For Leah to conceive, she had to be intimate with Jacob. For that intimacy to take place, there had to be a level of stillness and closeness. Conception requires intimacy! Intimacy can be experienced emotionally, intellectually, physically, experientially and spiritually. All these areas are important for human growth and development. True intimacy in a relationship requires both parties in the relationship to be all in and willing to compromise for the sake of the other person. As it is in the natural, so is it in the spiritual.

James 4:8 tells us to draw near to God and He will draw near to us. Closeness to God requires intimacy. You cannot get close to him without becoming intimate with him. When we walk in intimacy with God His promise of peace, love, joy, strength and hope will usher us into wanting to display the Fruits of the Spirit. True intimacy with God requires that we spend time with Him in prayer, in His Words and in worship. True intimacy means that we become still enough to hear what He has to say and still enough to be impregnated with his desires and promises. True intimacy with Christ means that we will draw near to him with a true heart that is not divided between the world and our Savior. True intimacy will drive us to pant after God just like the deer panteth for the water brook. True intimacy requires that our worship be authentic and ascend before God as a true smelling savor. Intimacy with God will give us an experience like the woman with the alabaster box of oil who left her fragrance of worship lingering with Christ. God is seeking to have an intimate relationship with us so He can place His desires in us so we can conceive and bring forth.

Prayer – Father I thank you that your Word tells me that if I draw near to you, you will draw near to me. My heart seeks and longs after you, Oh God. I thirst after you and long to be in your presence. Father, search my heart and see whatever wicked ways there be and cleanse me from all unrighteousness. I want to know you more. I want to know you in the fellowship of your suffering. Give me the desires of your heart and help me to seek after you with all my heart so I may experience true intimacy with you. In Jesus' name, amen.

Reflection

Intimacy With God

"Come close to God, and God will come close to you. Wash your hands, you sinners; purify your hearts, for your loyalty is divided between God and the world." (James 4:8, NLT)

What is God telling me today?

What am I praying for today?

A Heart of Gratitude

"Devote yourselves to prayer, being watchful and thankful." - Colossians 4:2 (NIV)

Today I am thankful for:

CONCEPTION

"So Leah conceived and bore a son..."- (Gen. 29:32, NKJV)

The word conceive carries different meanings based on how the word is being used. The Webster dictionary defines it as to become pregnant with (young); to cause to begin; to take into one's mind; to apprehend by reason or imagination and to have as an opinion. The bible said God opened Leah's womb and she conceived and bore a son. A seed was planted in her womb by Jacob and she became pregnant with something, a son! For this to happen, she had to be still enough for the seed to get into her womb and wait for the process of conception to take place.

God is waiting on us to be still enough so He can impregnate us with His will and His purpose. The egg was already in Leah, but she needed Jacob's seed to connect with her eggs and start the process of conception. God has already placed the seed on the inside of us. He is just waiting to have an intimate encounter with us so the process of conception can take place in us. Conception not only takes place in the womb, but it also takes place in our spirit, our heart, and in our mind. Whenever we conceive, something must come forth. It may not be a baby from our womb, but a manifestation must be brought forth. We may have conceived an idea in our mind that will allow us to devise a plan that will catapult us into purpose. We may have conceived something in our heart that will bring forth hope and help others to come to the saving knowledge of Christ. We may have conceived in our spirit and become pregnant with purpose and with a mission from God. As important as conception is, manifestation is equally as important because if God opened our wombs, hearts or minds and allowed us to conceive, He will finish what He started and allow the manifestation to come forth.

What is God opening your womb to conceive in this season? Remember, He had it shut and deliberately opened it so you can bring forth what He has placed in it. He has already given you the ability and the stamina to carry what He has placed in you. Genesis 1:11 states "Then God said, 'Let the earth bring forth grass, the herb that yields seed, and the fruit tree that yields fruit according to its kind, whose seed is in itself, on the earth': and it was so." The seed of what God wants you to bring forth has already been placed in you. Everything you need has already been placed inside you and is waiting to be revealed. Unlock your heart and your mind to line up with the Word and the will of God so you can bring forth what has been conceived in you. Allow God to work in and through you to bring what you are carrying to full maturity so He can get the glory and others may be blessed.

Prayer – Father I thank you for the ability to conceive. I thank you for allowing me to conceive and for giving me the ability to carry what you have placed in me to full maturity. Father your Word said the seed of anything is within itself. I declare that all the seeds that are already in me to bring forth will begin to grow and manifest itself. Help me to open my heart to be receptive to what you are doing in my life in this season and to be willing to carry what you have placed in me. In Jesus' name, amen.

Conception

"So Leah conceived and bore a son…" – (Gen. 29:32, NKJV)

What is God telling me today?

____

____

____

____

____

____

____

What am I praying for today?

____

____

____

____

____

____

____

____

A Heart of Gratitude

"Let the peace of Christ rule in your hearts, since as members of one body you were called to peace. And be thankful." – Colossians 3:15 (NIV)

Today I am thankful for:

WHAT AM I CARRYING?

"Three days later the Israelite officers went through the camp, giving these instructions to the people: 'When you see the Levitical priests carrying the Ark of the Covenant of the Lord your God, move out from your positions and follow them.'" (Josh. 3:2-3, NLT)

When I became pregnant with my daughter, I was so excited that I wanted to tell everyone I met that I was carrying a baby. I was not sure what sex the baby was going to be, but I was ecstatic that I was carrying a baby. During my pregnancy, I became more aware of what I was doing to my body, what I was eating, how much rest I was getting, and at times, who I was around. My pregnancy was classified as "high risk", and this meant my doctor's visits became more frequent and I had to follow his instructions more closely because I understood the nature of what can happen if I don't take the necessary precautions and follow strict orders.

In Joshua chapter 3, the Levitical Priests were carrying the Ark of the Covenant which represents the place where the Presence of God resides. They had to understand the significance and the importance of what they were carrying. While they were standing in Jordan, they had to be still amid the noise and chaos. People talking, babies crying, animals making noise; but that did not distract them from their assignments.

Leah was carrying a nation in her womb, but she did not recognize that because she was so distracted by her situation of being unloved. She had so much potential within her that was yet to be tapped into. God has placed so much potential within us that is untapped. We are carrying the ability to change a nation, change a generation, lead others to Christ, and change the trajectory of our lives. My potential is not what I have done, but what I have yet to do. The world is waiting on the gift that you are carrying, the YOU that nobody has seen before. The greatness that you have yet to attain is trapped inside you, and creation is waiting for you to bring it forth. The bible says out of your belly shall flow rivers of living water (John 7:38). God knows what He has given you the ability to carry, and He has placed everything within you to not only carry it, but also to bring it forth.

Don't settle for a community when God has given you nations. Let your dreams be bigger than your doubts. God knows what He has placed in you to carry.

What are you carrying? Are you burdened with what you are carrying? Matthew 11:29 says, "Simply join your life with mine. Learn my ways and you'll discover that I'm gentle, humble, easy to please. You will find refreshment and rest in me" (TPT). Are you carrying unforgiveness? Ephesians 4:32 says, "But instead be kind and affectionate toward one another. Has God graciously forgiven you? Then graciously forgive one another in the depths of Christ's love" (TPT). Are you carrying guilt and shame? Romans 8:1 says, "So now the case is closed. There remains no accusing voice of condemnation against those who are joined in life-union with Jesus, the Anointed One" (TPT). What you are carrying does not get canceled because of a mistake you may have made. Give yourself permission to trust God and know that what He started in you He will finish. Know that you will carry out the assignment that is within you, the nations will benefit from what you are carrying, and God will be glorified through its completion. Be assured that whatever you are carrying, God will carry you through the process.

Prayer – Father in the name of Jesus, I thank you for all my God-given potential. I thank you for trusting me to carry the assignment you have placed in me. Holy Spirit teach me to be sincere and understand the importance and the significance of what I am carrying. Help me not to take my assignment for granted, but to trust you in the process that all things will work together for my good because I trust you and because I am in Christ Jesus. Give me clarity for my assignment. Give me insight, wisdom, knowledge and understanding of how to carry it and execute it so the Father may be glorified. In Jesus' name, amen.

What Am I Carrying?

"Three days later the Israelite officers went through the camp, giving these instructions to the people: 'When you see the Levitical priests carrying the Ark of the Covenant of the Lord your God, move out from your positions and follow them.'" (Josh. 3:2-3, NLT)

What is God telling me today?

What am I praying for today?

A Heart of Gratitude

"So then, just as you received Christ Jesus as Lord, continue to live your lives in him, rooted and built up in him, strengthened in the faith as you were taught, and overflowing with thankfulness." - Colossians 2:6-7(NIV)

Today I am thankful for:

BIRTHING RUBEN

"So Leah conceived and bore a son, and she called his name Reuben; for she said, 'The LORD has surely looked on my affliction. Now therefore, my husband will love me.'" (Gen. 29:32, NKJV)

Several weeks into my pregnancy, I found out that I was carrying a precious baby girl. I named her Davena Angelica which means beloved messenger. Her first name was the female version of her dad's name; David. Her middle name came from my middle name Angela. I wanted to make sure there was some significance to what her name was and what it meant.

God opened Leah's womb and she gave birth to a son and called him Reuben. The name Reuben meant "the Lord has seen my affliction". God did see Leah's affliction because He opened her womb when he saw that she was unloved. Even though she felt afflicted, God still allowed her to conceive and bring forth a son.

God can and will use us during our season of affliction. Don't allow the enemy or anyone to allow you to believe that God cannot use you because you have been afflicted. God is purposeful and intentional in what He does and what He allows to happen to His children. Psalms 119:71 says, "It was good for me to be afflicted so that I might learn your decrees." Afflictions can bring out the best or the worst in us. David acknowledges that because of him being afflicted, he was forced to learn the ways of God. Affliction will sometimes pull us closer to God. It will keep us from becoming prideful and acknowledge that we would not have made it if God were not on our side. Affliction will steer us to be dependent on God. Psalms 25:16 says "Turn to me and be gracious to me, for I am lonely and afflicted." Affliction will remind us that God has not forgotten us and that His grace is sufficient for us. It allows us to recognize that during our time of weakness, God's strength is made perfect in us according to 2 Corinthians 12:9.

Leah was not totally convinced that God was working on her behalf. She was still struck by the fact that Jacob still did not love her as he ought to. She failed to realize that God was giving her the love that Jacob was unable to give her. Are you so wounded by your affliction that you cannot see that God is working on your behalf or that He loves you with an everlasting love? God sees and knows all. His love for you is unquestionable. He wants you to give Him the opportunity to allow Him to display His love and power in and through you.

Prayer – Father, I thank you for seeing my affliction and helping me to have the victory. Lord your Word said had I not been afflicted; I would not have learned your ways. Help me to learn and observe your way in my times of affliction. Help me to know that my affliction is only for a season, and you will give me the strength to make it through. Teach me how to lean and depend on you during my affliction so your strength can be made perfect during my weakness. I thank you for using me even while I am afflicted. In Jesus' name, amen.

Birthing Ruben

"So Leah conceived and bore a son, and she called his name Reuben; for she said, 'The LORD has surely looked on my affliction. Now therefore, my husband will love me.'"- (Gen. 29:32, NKJV)

What is God telling me today?

What am I praying for today?

A Heart of Gratitude

"Always giving thanks to God the Father for everything, in the name of our Lord Jesus Christ."- Ephesians 5:20(NIV)

Today I am thankful for:

Day 10

BIRTHING SIMEON

"Then she conceived again and bore a son, and said, 'Because the LORD has heard that I am unloved, He has therefore given me this son also.' And she called his name Simeon." (Gen. 29: 33, NKJV)

What do we do when God gives us another chance to acknowledge who He is and what He has done in our life, and we are still unable to do so? What happens when we refuse to see His hands and not the hands of man at work in our situation? God continued to pour out His blessings on Leah. He was fulfilling His perfect will for her life, but it was hard for her to see because once again she was consumed with her Jacob situation. Leah was on a journey of becoming and God was processing her for what was to come.

She conceived again and called her son Simeon. The name means that God has heard her cry of being and feeling unloved. When you are being processed for greatness, sometimes being unloved by others will be a part of the journey. Sometimes you will be unloved by people because they are jealous of what you are carrying or what you have given birth to. God will allow what you are carrying to be manifested in the presence of those by whom you are unloved. You did not give birth to Simeon because you are unloved, you gave birth to Simeon because God allowed you to do so. Don't allow the way you feel to get in the way of what God is doing in your life.

Do you believe that God hears your cry? Do you believe that He will deliver you? What are you fearful of? Psalms 34:6 tells us that He not only hears our cry, but He also delivers us from our troubles and from fear. Just as how God heard Leah's cry, He also hears your cry. Is there anything too hard for God? Absolutely not! His ears are not deaf unto our cry, and He cares about what we are going through. I want to admonish you to trust in the Lord and what He is doing in your life. Keep your eyes fixed on Him regardless of how you may be feeling. Feeling unloved is never a good feeling, but know that the King of the universe loves you unconditionally and He hears you each time that you call.

Prayer – Holy Spirit thank you for reminding me that I am loved unconditionally by my Father, God. Sometimes that love feels like it's so far away. Remind me that you are only a breath away and your loving arms are wrapped around me even when I don't feel it. Thank you for loving me so much that you sent your son to die for me. When I feel unloved, remind me of your word in Romans 5:8 which tells me, "But God demonstrates his own love for us in this: While we were still sinners, Christ died for us". Thank you for demonstrating your love. In Jesus' name, amen.

Birthing Simeon

"Then she conceived again and bore a son, and said, 'Because the LORD has heard that I am unloved, He has therefore given me this son also.' And she called his name Simeon."- (Gen. 29: 33, NKJV)

What is God telling me today?

____

____

____

____

____

____

____

What am I praying for today?

____

____

____

____

____

____

____

____

A Heart of Gratitude

"We always thank God for all of you and continually mention you in our prayers. We remember before our God and Father your work produced by faith, your labor prompted by love, and your endurance inspired by hope in our Lord Jesus Christ."- 1 Thessalonians 1:2-3 (NIV)

Today I am thankful for:

BIRTHING LEVI

"She conceived again and bore a son, and said, 'Now this time my husband will become attached to me, because I have borne him three sons.' Therefore, his name was called Levi."- (Gen. 29:34, NKJV)

The word attach can mean to connect; to place so as to belong; to assign by authority; to appoint. It also means to be connected by ties of love; to attract or fasten by moral influence. I remember a season in my life that I was attached to the wrong person because he had a love for music the way I do, and I was attracted to what he was doing in the natural.

Leah conceived a third time and again she gave birth to another son and named him based on how she was feeling. She called him Levi because she thought this time for sure Jacob was going to attach himself to her because she gave him a third son. What was Leah trying to gain? She was trying to connect or fasten herself to someone who did not have the concept of what true love is? Jacob was in love with the outward appearance of Rachel's beauty, but was unable to see past Leah's exterior flaws. He had no insight into what was within her. There are people in your life who are stuck on what they can see on the outside of you and are unaware of what God is doing in you.

Leah was longing to be loved by Jacob so much that she was willing to attach herself to someone that God did not give her permission to become attached to. The pain of being unloved was so evident in her heart that she was willing to sacrifice her self-worth for someone who could not love her the way Christ did. She was so focused on the external love of Jacob that she was still missing the process of what God was doing in her life. She was willing to be attached in the natural and miss what was happening in the spirit realm because her heart was so broken.

Are you missing out on what God is doing in your life because you are attached to the wrong person or the wrong thing? Are you attached emotionally or spiritually to people or things that God did not assign you to? If you are, stop attaching yourself to people who are not a part of your destiny. Be willing to detach yourself and know that God will attach you to those who He has ordained to be a part of your destiny, those that He has assigned to deposit in your life and those who can help you in the process of birthing. Don't attach yourself to people or things that cannot see or be a part of what God is doing in your life in this season.

Are you so focused on the pain that you cannot see the process of the healing that is taking place? Give yourself permission to be healed and allow God to begin the process of healing in you. The

bible tells us that "The Lord is close to the brokenhearted and saves those who are crushed in spirit" (Psalm 34:18). Open your heart and allow God to heal your hurt. Jesus suffered a broken heart when he was battered, betrayed, abandoned, and rejected. He came out victorious and you can too. Psalms 147:3 tells us that he heals the brokenhearted and bandages up their wounds. He is closer to you than you realize and is waiting with open arms to heal your broken heart and bandage ALL your wounds.

Prayer – Father, I release all my hurt and brokenness to you today. I will not carry them anymore. I declare that as of today, my heart is healed, and I am walking in your total wholeness because you came to give me life and to give it to me in abundance. I thank you for my healing and for those that you have placed in my life to assist me in walking in my place of healing. In Jesus' name, amen.

Reflection

Birthing Levi

"She conceived again and bore a son, and said, 'Now this time my husband will become attached to me, because I have borne him three sons.' Therefore, his name was called Levi."- (Gen. 29:34, NKJV)

What is God telling me today?

____

____

____

____

____

____

____

What am I praying for today?

____

____

____

____

____

____

____

____

A Heart of Gratitude

"I always thank my God for you because of his grace given you in Christ Jesus." - 1 Corinthians 1:4 (NIV)

Today I am thankful for:

BIRTHING JUDAH

"And she conceived again and bore a son, and said, 'Now I will praise the LORD.' Therefore, she called his name Judah. Then she stopped bearing." (Gen. 29:35, NKJV)

What happens when God continually blesses you and you are unaware because you are so caught up in what you are going through? I have been there! I have been so distracted by my situation and what happened in my past that I neglected to see what God was doing in the now.

Leah spent so much time reminiscing about what was happening that she missed so many opportunities to thank the one blessing her for the blessings. Sometimes we are so blinded by what has happened to us that we cannot see that God is trying to move us beyond our past.

God allowed Leah to conceive again and this time something in her caught a glimpse of what God was doing and she named her child Judah which means praise. She gave birth to the promise! The promise that was sent to deliver mankind from their sin. Leah was no longer focused on what Jacob could not do for her but on what God was doing in her. She declared that "this time I will praise the Lord!" She seems determined not to allow the circumstances that got

Her to where she was to become her present situation. The bible said Leah stopped bearing or having children. It does not mean that she no longer had the ability to have more children, it just meant that her pain stopped once she started praising God.

Praise became an expression of Leah's testimony. David said in Psalms "my soul shall boast in the Lord". We must be willing to showcase our expression of praise no matter what we are going through. We should never allow our situation or circumstances to dictate our level of praise or worship. We must be willing to praise God in spite of our situation or our circumstance. When we open our mouth and praise God, it shows our admiration for God. When we praise Him, it becomes an act of our will. God is worthy of our praise at all times. Praise is not something we do when we feel like it. It should be a part of our everyday life. Psalms 34:1 says "I will praise the Lord at all times. I will constantly speak of His praises" (NLT). We ought to praise God when we feel like it and most importantly, when we don't feel like it. Praising Him when we don't feel like it will silence the enemy. Praise is a weapon that is available to the children of God to defeat the enemy. Let praise become an expression of your faith. Use your weapon!

Prayer – Father, my soul magnifies you. I praise you for who you are. Help me to praise you in spite of my situation and my circumstances. Help me not to focus on the magnitude of my situation, but on the magnitude of my God. I praise you because you are marvelous. I praise you because you are excellent. I praise you because you are the Omnipotent, Omniscient and Omnipresent God. I thank you for the ability to praise you. In Jesus' name, amen.

Reflection

Birthing Judah

"And she conceived again and bore a son, and said, 'Now I will praise the LORD.' Therefore, she called his name Judah. Then she stopped bearing." (Gen. 29:35, NKJV)

What is God telling me today?

____

____

____

____

____

____

____

What am I praying for today?

____

____

____

____

____

____

____

____

A Heart of Gratitude

"Therefore, since we are receiving a kingdom that cannot be shaken, let us be thankful, and so worship God acceptably with reverence and awe, for our God is a consuming fire." - Hebrews 12:28-29 (NIV)

Today I am thankful for:

FROM PAIN TO PURPOSE

"And she conceived again and bore a son, and said, 'Now I will praise the LORD.' Therefore, she called his name Judah. Then she stopped bearing." - (Gen. 29:35, NKJV)

Several years ago, I had the awesome opportunity of ministering in Australia. During my time there, I was invited to speak during a Sunday morning service. While getting prepared, I started to experience excruciating pain in my back. The pain became so unbearable that I thought I would not be able to deliver the message that God had given to me. Upon pushing my way through the pain, ministering and doing an altar call, I realized the pain had stopped. I then realized that the pain was trying to keep me from walking into the purpose of what I was assigned to do that morning.

Having a revelation of where God is taking us is very important. However, having the revelation of the destination, but no insight of the journey can be painful. Leah's journey to birthing out purpose was not without pain. She experienced the pain of being unloved, the pain of not being noticed by her husband, the pain of being judged based on what others think, and the pain of being labeled because of her situation of not looking like what others believe she should look like.

What if Leah had decided not to be intimate with Jacob because she was unloved? A nation would not have come forth from her womb. We cannot make decisions based on how we feel or where we are. God was doing something in Leah's life, and she had to realize that the manifestation was important, but the process to get to the manifestation was critical. Sometimes pain is so unbearable that we learn to appreciate the value of what comes out of the pain.

When God is birthing purpose through us, we have to go through a process. Just like birthing is a process; so is manifestation. We must be willing to endure the process. We cannot abandon the process of going through pregnancy because we want to see the baby. If I abandon the process, I will not see the manifestation. I must be committed to the process for purpose to come forth. Sometimes our process can be so painful that we want to stop short of the promise. 1 Peter 5:10 tells us that after you have suffered a little while, the God of all grace who called us to His eternal glory by Christ Jesus will perfect, establish, strengthen and settle you. God transitioned Leah from pain to purpose and He is waiting to do the same for you. Allow Him to take you through the process so purpose can come forth. Always remember that your purpose is greater than your pain.

Prayer – Father, I thank you that purpose was placed in me before the foundation of the world. You told Jeremiah that you knew him before he was formed in his mother's womb. I am thankful that you also knew me and placed everything in me that I needed to walk in my purpose. Lord sometimes when the pain is unbearable, it feels like purpose is never going to come forth. Help me to push pass the past so purpose can be birthed. Thank you for reminding me that my purpose is greater than my pain. In Jesus' name, amen.

From Pain To Purpose

"And she conceived again and bore a son, and said, 'Now I will praise the LORD.' Therefore, she called his name Judah. Then she stopped bearing." - (Gen. 29:35, NKJV)

What is God telling me today?

What am I praying for today?

A Heart of Gratitude

"I urge, then, first of all, that petitions, prayers, intercession and thanksgiving be made for all people."- 1 Timothy 2:1-2 (NIV)

Today I am thankful for:

SPIRITUAL MIDWIFE

"When Leah saw that she had stopped bearing, she took Zilpah her maid and gave her to Jacob as his wife. (Gen. 30:9, KJV)

When I was giving birth to my daughter, I had my doctor, my husband, and a few nurses in the room with me. The doctor and some of the nurses that were there assisted in the birthing and my husband and my mother were there for moral support. The pain I was feeling clouded my mind to everything else. The job of the nurses was crucial because they told me when to push and this helped the momentum by letting me know I was capable of birthing my daughter.

The bible said when Leah stopped bearing, she gave her handmaiden Zilpah to Jacob so she could conceive and bring forth a child for her. The name Zilpah means "uncertain". Have you ever had those seasons in your life where you knew God had placed something in you and you were uncertain about how you would carry out that assignment? You were even uncertain about whether you had the capacity to carry the assignment. God is so intentional about what He wants that He will position midwives in our lives to carry for us what we may not have the strength to carry. He will place midwives in our lives to help us carry the load when it becomes unbearable. Zilpah gave birth to a son named Gad which means "fortune". The situation that you felt uncertain about or that place of uncertainty where you may be, God can turn your situation around and cause fortune to come out of that situation and from that place when you least expect it. Don't put limits on God. Don't push away the people that He may be sending in your life to become midwives and help you bring forth in your season of uncertainty.

I declared that you would bring what you are carrying to full maturity and that God will send the right midwife in your season to help you push past the pain and encourage you to hold fast, be steadfast and unmovable as you deliver what He has placed in your womb. 2 Peter 3:9 tells us that God is not slack concerning His promises. He will bring to pass that which he promises.

Prayer – Father, I thank you for the Zilpah that you have placed in my life at one time or another to assist me in carrying out my assignments. Help me to understand their purpose and to not push them away because I am unaware or unable to see instant manifestation. I thank you for aligning me with the right midwife who will be aligned with my purpose and understand what you are doing in my life at the time you place them there. Thank you for the ones who will help to pull me out of my dry places. I thank you for giving me the right temperament to deal with my midwives. In Jesus' name. amen.

Spiritual Midwife

"When Leah saw that she had stopped bearing, she took Zilpah her maid and gave her to Jacob as his wife."- (Gen. 30:9, KJV)

What is God telling me today?

____

____

____

____

____

____

____

What am I praying for today?

____

____

____

____

____

____

____

____

A Heart of Gratitude

"Do not be anxious about anything, but in every situation, by prayer and petition, with thanksgiving, present your requests to God. And the peace of God, which transcends all understanding, will guard your hearts and your minds in Christ Jesus."- Philippians 4:6-7 (NIV)

Today I am thankful for:

THE PROCESS

"We do this by keeping our eyes on Jesus, the champion who initiates and perfects our faith. Because of the joy awaiting him, he endured the cross, disregarding its shame. Now he is seated in the place of honor beside God's throne." (Heb. 12:2, NLT)

Just about everything we do in the natural requires us to go through a process. Sometimes the process can be so painful that we want to give up and not accomplish the purpose. When I gave birth to this message, I was in great emotional, spiritual, and financial pain. I was uncertain about what to do and which direction to go in. I had walked away from my job of 14 years to start a business that never materialized even though I put so much effort into it. I had one plan, but God had another. His plan brought me into places I would have never been able to go to had I been working. I did not understand the process of the pain because I could not see the destination.

The book of Hebrews talked about Jesus enduring the pain because He knew that as painful as the cross was, the joy of bringing salvation to a dying world was more joyful. He pushed past the pain and the shame so you and I can have life and have it more abundantly.

The process of birthing is never easy. You must go through different stages of pregnancy before the baby comes forth. After going

through the process of carrying the baby for a period, you then have to endure the task of laboring for what you have been carrying to come forth. You go through contractions and dilating which can be very painful and yet the baby is just preparing to come, but still in the womb. Sometimes in the spirit we feel the push and the pull of what God is calling us to, and yet He may be saying it's still not time. Make sure you are allowing yourself to go through the process so what you are carrying does not come forth prematurely.

What are you carrying that you feel like it's taking too long, or you cannot bear the pain anymore? Could it be that God is processing you for greater? Allow Him to see you through the process. If you abort the process, you will never see the result of what you are carrying. Don't allow the pain of the journey to stop you from getting to your destination. Psalms 30:5 says "Weeping may endure for a night, but joy is cometh in the morning." Endure the process because the manifestation will be greater than the pain.

Prayer – Father, I trust you in this season to take me through the process so I can get to the destination. Sometimes the journey is painful, but I know with you in the boat with me, I can smile at the storm. Teach me how to take your yoke because it is light and to release all my burdens to you. I know that as painful as my journey may be, the joy of knowing that you are with me makes the pain easier to bear. Thank you for being my burden bearer. In Jesus' name, amen.

Reflection

The Process

"We do this by keeping our eyes on Jesus, the champion who initiates and perfects our faith. Because of the joy awaiting him, he endured the cross, disregarding its shame. Now he is seated in the place of honor beside God's throne." (Heb. 12:2, NLT)

What is God telling me today?

____

____

____

____

____

____

____

What am I praying for today?

____

____

____

____

____

____

____

____

A Heart of Gratitude

"All this is for your benefit, so that the grace that is reaching more and more people may cause thanksgiving to overflow to the glory of God." - 2 Corinthians 4:15

Today I am thankful for:

POSTURE FOR BIRTHING

"So Ahab went up to eat and drink. And Elijah went up to the top of Carmel; then he bowed down on the ground and put his face between his knees." (1 Kings 18:42, NKJV)

The process of giving birth is hard work! It is called "labor" for good reason. One of the Webster revised dictionary definitions of labor is "That which requires hard work for its accomplishment; that which demands effort". Giving birth not only requires great effort on the part of the one giving birth, but it also requires for that individual to be in the right posture and the right frame of mind.

Research shows that there are several different positions that can be used when giving birth. Dr. Sara Twogood stated that "Rotating between different labor and birthing positions is important to optimize conditions for the mom and baby." There are some positions that will allow the mother to be more comfortable but may cause complications for the baby and may not be recommended for all mothers.

As it is in the natural, so it is in the spiritual. When God gives us an assignment, it may require us to posture ourselves a certain way in order to see the manifestation of that spoken word. The bible talks

about Elijah who God gave a word that it was going to rain. He did not sit back and wait for it to rain; he postured himself with his face between his knees and cried out to God for the manifestation of what He told him. Elijah's posture denotes giving birth. It had not rained in three years and the people as well as the land were desperate. He was willing to change position and travail to see and move the hand of God for the rain to come.

Leah may not have changed her posture for birthing, but she had to change her mindset and her approach to her situation. After she changed her mindset, her situation changed, and she saw a greater purpose to give God praise.

What are you believing God for today? What word has He spoken to you, and you are yet to see the manifestation of that spoken word? What prophetic word have you been given that seems to be held up? Are you willing to change your position and posture yourself to see God move? Trust God to move on your behalf. Allow your faith to go before your problems and watch God move.

Prayer – Father, I thank you for giving me the strength and the wisdom to change my position and get in the right posture to see your manifestation. Holy Spirit help me to take you at your word and believe that whatever you say will come to pass. In Jesus' name, amen.

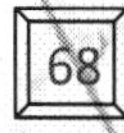

Posture For Birthing

"So Ahab went up to eat and drink. And Elijah went up to the top of Carmel; then he bowed down on the ground and put his face between his knees." - (1 Kings 18:42, NKJV)

What is God telling me today?

What am I praying for today?

A Heart of Gratitude

"Give thanks to the Lord, for he is good. For His lovingkindness (graciousness, mercy, compassion) endures forever."- Psalm 136:1(AMP)

Today I am thankful for:

PREPARATION FOR BIRTHING

"Go to the ant, O sluggard; consider her ways, and be wise. Without having any chief, officer, or ruler, she prepares her bread in summer and gathers her food in harvest." (Prov. 6:6-8, ESV)

My preparation process for birthing my daughter was something we had to do if we wanted to be prepared for her coming into this world. We had to buy clothing, we had to get her room ready, we had to make sure she had a car seat to be placed in when she left the hospital. So as it is in the natural, so it is in the spiritual realm. We cannot expect to bring forth in the spirit realm without proper preparation. Sometimes we said we are waiting on God; when He is actually waiting on us to get prepared. What we are carrying is too important for us not to be prepared for what is coming.

The dictionary definition of preparation is: a proceeding, measure, or provision by which one prepares for something: any proceeding, experience, or the like considered as a mode of preparing for the future. I cannot give birth if I am not prepared! Jesus had to be prepared for the journey of going to the cross. David had to be prepared to take the throne as King of Israel. Abraham had to be prepared to be the father of many nations by leaving his place of comfort so he could walk into the promised land and give birth to what God had promised. John the Baptist prepared the way for the coming of Christ. The bible tells us that even the ants with no ruler over it, prepares in the summer so it can have food in the winter. If this is done naturally, how much more should we be prepared for what God is getting ready to birth out of us.

How do I get prepared? Getting prepared means that I must spend time in the Word of God. It means I must spend time in the Presence of God. It means my ear must be so close to his mouth that I do not miss what He is saying to do.

In preparing for birthing, my posture must be correct. A woman cannot give birth without being opened. Even if it's a c-section, her womb must be opened. We cannot expect to bring forth what God has placed in us if we are not in the right posture. Gideon had to test the posture of the men he was going into battle with to see who was really ready for war.

What is your posture for birthing? Are you ready to bring forth? Are you beginning to feel the pressure of what you are carrying and know that you need to position yourself for what is coming? God is waiting on you! Are you ready?

Prayer – Holy Spirit, I thank you for giving me the strength and the tenacity to endure every process in my life. If I am not in the correct posture, reposition me for what is coming. At times, it seems insurmountable, and I sometimes feel as if I will not make it to my destination. Your word told me that you have given me everything that I need both spiritually and naturally and I declare that I will trust you in the process because I will make it to the destination you have prepared for me. In Jesus' name, amen.

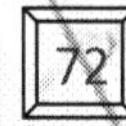

Preparation For Birthing

"Go to the ant, O sluggard; consider her ways, and be wise. Without having any chief, officer, or ruler, she prepares her bread in summer and gathers her food in harvest."- (Prov. 6:6-8, ESV)

What is God telling me today?

What am I praying for today?

A Heart of Gratitude

"Give thanks to the Lord, for he is good; his love endures forever."- Psalms 118:29 (NIV)

Today I am thankful for:

THE IMPACT OF MY SEED.

"At the sound of Mary's greeting, Elizabeth's child leaped within her, and Elizabeth was filled with the Holy Spirit."- (Luke 1:41, NIV)

When I became pregnant with my son, I had a hard time gaining weight and my doctor was very worried about me. He thought I was not caring much for myself and the baby I was carrying and felt I needed counseling. I was aware of what I was carrying, but had some symptoms that left me not feeling too excited about my pregnancy. Sometimes when God plant seeds in our womb the impact from carrying it can cause us to lose sight of what is to come forth from the seed because the journey towards the manifestation of the seed may be painful.

The bible said that Elizabeth was pregnant, and Mary went to pay her a visit. However, Elizabeth was unaware that Mary was not only pregnant, but she was carrying the child Christ. The Savior of the world. The one who came to bring not only joy to the world, but most importantly –salvation. What Mary was carrying was so important and significant that it impacted what was on the inside of Elizabeth and caused her baby to leap.

Leah did not understand how impactful her birthing would be to the world. She had no idea that what she was carrying would affect the world and impact the Kingdom of God. Would her demeanor towards what she was birthing out be different had she known? Sometimes when God plants a seed on the inside of us, we are not sure what will come forth and sometimes when the journey seems too tumultuous, we want to stop short of the birthing or even try to abort what we are carrying.

Philippians 1:6: states, "I pray with great faith for you, because I'm fully convinced that the One who began this glorious work in you will faithfully continue the process of maturing you and will put his finishing touches to it until the unveiling of our Lord Jesus Christ!" (TPT). God is not slack concerning His promises. He will see you through. Trust Him!

Prayer – Father, thank you for the seed of what I am carrying. Sometimes the enemy wants me to believe I don't have the capacity to carry what you placed with me. I declare that what has been planted in my womb will come forth in due season and will impact nations for the Glory of God. In Jesus' name, amen.

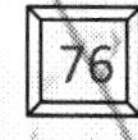

The Impact of My Seed

"At the sound of Mary's greeting, Elizabeth's child leaped within her, and Elizabeth was filled with the Holy Spirit."- (Luke 1:41, NIV)

What is God telling me today?

____

____

____

____

____

____

____

What am I praying for today?

____

____

____

____

____

____

____

____

A Heart of Gratitude

"Open for me the gates of the righteous; I will enter and give thanks to the Lord."- Psalm 118:19 (NIV)

Today I am thankful for:

BIRTHING ISSACHAR

"And God is able to make all grace abound to you, so that in all things, at all times, having all that you need, you will abound in every good work."
(2 Cor. 9:8, KVJ)

Have you ever been labeled by others? Have you ever felt less than because someone used their words to describe who they think you are? I have been there! I have been labeled because I did not look like someone else, did not shape or sound like someone else.

Issachar whose name came from the Hebrew word yissakar means "he will bring a reward." The root word from his name which came from "nasa" means "to lift, to advance, arise, bring forth, raise up. It is said he was destined for a life of hard labor. Even though he was labeled, he did not allow his future to be defined by what others said. The sons of Issachar had a great assignment, they walked in an anointing that allowed them to discern times and seasons. They also had the intuition of knowing what to do during those seasons. Because of the anointing on their lives, they were well respected and were used to study the stars and create annual calendars.

Psalms 139:14 declares "I will praise You, for I am fearfully and wonderfully made; Marvelous are Your works". When we were created by God, He predestined what and who we become. Our destinies are not determined by man. God will cause you to be lifted up before those that label you. He will raise you up for others to see that He had a great plan for your life regardless of how they labeled you. God is the final storyteller. He predestined us from the very foundation of the world, and He gets the glory. When God's hands are upon you, it does not matter what others believe you should be doing or should become; what God has is for you!

Prayer – Father, I thank you for fearfully and wonderfully creating me. I thank you that even if I don't seem marvelous in the eyes of others, you see me as being marvelous because I am your creation. I thank you for creating me with care and with great love. In Jesus' name, amen.

Birthing Issachar

"And God is able to make all grace abound to you, so that in all things, at all times, having all that you need, you will abound in every good work." (2 Cor. 9:8, KJV)

What is God telling me today?

What am I praying for today?

A Heart of Gratitude

"Let them give thanks to the Lord for his unfailing love and his wonderful deeds for mankind."- Psalm 107:8 (NIV)

Today I am thankful for:

THE BLESSINGS OF BIRTHING PRAISE

"I will praise the Lord at all times. I will constantly speak his praises. I will boast only in the Lord; let all who are helpless take heart. Come, let us tell of the Lord's greatness; let us exalt his name together." - *(Psalm 34:1-3, NLT)*

Have you ever experienced the joy of praising God in spite of? I am not talking about the kind of praise you do because God did something great for you or because you received a new car or house. Not the praise where a situation arises, and you knew how you were going to overcome it. I am talking about the kind of praise you do when your back is up against the wall, and you don't know what to do. The kind of praise you do when your situation looks dim, and it seems like you are not going to find a way out of it. The praise that you do in spite of! The praise that causes you to do what Paul and Silas did so you can experience chains breaking and falling off.

Judah, the praise that came forth out of Leah, gave birth to several sons who walked in their own blessings because they came forth from praise. Isaiah 25:1 declares, "I will exalt you and praise your name, for in perfect faithfulness you have done wonderful things, things planned long ago." When we allow praise to be born out of our spirit, we get to experience the mighty hands of God. We get to see God move in our situation. We get to witness the manifested glory and power of God in our life. Birthing praise even when you are in pain will move the hands of God to come through for you. He is a God that honors sacrifices, and He will honor your praise when it is authentic and coming from within your spirit. Isaiah 43:2 says, "When you pass through the waters, I will be with you; and when you pass through the rivers, they will not sweep over you. When you walk through the fire, you will not be burned; the flames will not set you ablaze."

Isaiah 43:2 is God's guarantee that He will be with us. Praise Him while you are going through the waters and the fire and watch Him come through. Learn how to praise Him IN SPITE OF!

Prayer – Holy Spirit teach me how to praise you in spite of. I praise you not for what you can give me, but because you are God and beside you there is no other. I praise you because you are great and mighty. I praise you because your Word tells me, "let everything that hath breathe praise the Lord". Father I will praise you even as I pass through the water and the fire because your Word tells me that it will not sweep over me and I will not be burned. Thank you for lending me the breath to praise you continually. In Jesus' name, amen.

Reflection

The Blessings of Birthing Praise

"I will praise the Lord at all times. I will constantly speak his praises. I will boast only in the Lord; let all who are helpless take heart. Come, let us tell of the Lord's greatness; let us exalt his name together."(Psalm 34:1-3, NLT)

What is God telling me today?

What am I praying for today?

A Heart of Gratitude

"Praise the Lord. Give thanks to the Lord, for he is good; his love endures forever."- Psalm 106:1(NIV)

Today I am thankful for:

TAKE THE LIMITS OFF

"And the God of all grace, who called you to His eternal glory in Christ, after you have suffered a little while, will Himself restore you and make you strong, firm and steadfast." - (1 Peter 5:10, NIV)

Have you ever lost anything? Have you ever had to give up something that meant a lot to you? Well, if you have, join the club! The Lord blessed my husband and I with what I called my dream home. The house was everything I'd wanted in a home and when we had to walk away from it, I had an extremely hard time accepting it. It took me a few years to realize that I was placing a limit on God and not believing that He had the ability to return what I lost two-fold. If He did it for Job, He will do it for us. When Leah took the limit off God, she was able to experience joy and His glory.

Judah had five sons and two died. His remaining sons were, Shelah's whose name meant "Break away"; Perez meant "bring forth, breakthrough" and Zerah meant "rise up." When we place limits on God, we miss out on the opportunity to see Him move in our lives. God is calling us to break out of where we are because our breakthrough is closer than we think. He is calling us to rise up and take the limits off because the bible tells us in Ephesians 3:20 that

He can do exceedingly, abundantly more than we can even ask or think. What are you believing in Him for today? Have you placed a limit on what He can do for you? Break out and break free from the bondage of not enough and allow God to move you into your place of more than enough. He's calling us to press beyond our own limits and then we will be able to appreciate what can come forth from pressing. Take the limits off and just trust Him!

Prayer – Father, help me to take you at your word. Your word said you can do more than I can ask or think according to the power that is at work in me. Help me to realize that the power that is at work in me has no limit and therefore, I should not place a limit on you. In Jesus' name, amen.

Take The Limits Off

"And the God of all grace, who called you to his eternal glory in Christ, after you have suffered a little while, will himself restore you and make you strong, firm and steadfast."- (1 Peter 5:10, NIV)

What is God telling me today?

What am I praying for today?

A Heart of Gratitude

"Enter his gates with thanksgiving and his courts with praise; give thanks to him and praise his name."- Psalm 100:4 (NIV)

Today I am thankful for:

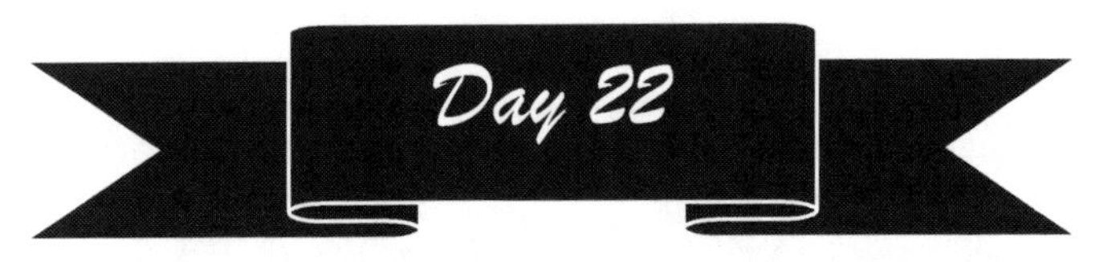

IT'S OK NOT TO BE OK!

"Why am I discouraged? Why is my heart so sad? I will put my hope in God! I will praise him again— my Savior and my God!"- (Psalm 43:5, NLT)

As children of God, we are led to believe that we must always exude joy. When asked how we are doing, we have developed the habit of responding "fine" or as some would say, "blessed". I went through a season in my life where I was watching a talk show and realized that I was in a state of depression and not admitting it. After talking with someone and admitting that I was in that state and seeking possible help, I realized that it was ok not to be ok.

Leah experienced many seasons of not being ok because Jacob showed no love towards her. The bible said when Jesus knew his time was drawing near for him to go to the cross, He prayed and asked the Father to take it away from Him, but He knew that it was not His will that needed to be in control but the will of the Father. David cried out in Psalm 43:5 asking himself why he was feeling so discouraged and why his heart was sad. He realized that he needed to put his hope in the King of Kings and Lord of Lords and praise him through his situation.

When you find yourself in that place of not being ok, talk to someone. Seek help from a professional if the need arises, but do not feel that you are alone or you should not feel that way. Reach out for help and turn to God because He can restore the joy of your salvation. The bible tells us in Hebrews 4:15 that we have a High Priest that is touched with the feelings of our infirmities. Just like he heard the cry of Leah and so many others, He will hear your cry. Reach out and touch Him. He is only a prayer away and is waiting with open arms to wrap His loving arms around you.

Prayer – Father, I thank you that when my soul is discouraged, I can turn to you because you are the author and the finisher of my faith. I thank you in those moments when I am not feeling ok, I can turn to you for your love and your comfort. I can turn to your Word and find strength. Thank you for being my strong tower and my refugee. In Jesus' name, amen.

It's OK not to be OK

"Why am I discouraged? Why is my heart so sad? I will put my hope in God! I will praise him again– my Savior and my God!"– (Psalm 43:5, NLT)

What is God telling me today?

What am I praying for today?

A Heart of Gratitude

"Give thanks to the Lord, for he is good; his love endures forever."- 1 Chronicles 16:34 (NIV)

Today I am thankful for:

WHAT SEASON AM I IN?

"But they who wait for the Lord shall renew their strength; they shall mount up with wings like eagles; they shall run and not be weary; they shall walk and not faint." - (Isaiah 40:31, ESE)

As women, sometimes when we are pregnant we get anxious because we want the journey to come to an end so we can see the manifestation of what we are carrying. Knowing our season is so important to what God is doing in our lives.

In birthing, the first stage is labor where we feel the pain but we are still not ready. Make sure you are not pushing before you enter your season for pushing. The active labor stage is when the cervix begins to open to reveal what you have been carrying. God is opening your womb to bring forth greatness. Allow Him to do the work as you wait on Him. The next stage which is the transition phase can be very intense and what you are carrying will begin to become more pressuring and you will have the overwhelming desire to push. The more intense the pressure, the quicker the birth.

What has God placed in you that you are beginning to feel the weight of it? Are you feeling the pressure to begin pushing? Are you now in your transitional stage where you know you have labored and waited on the Lord, and He has brought you to your season of manifestation? Are you positioned for birthing? If you believe your season has not yet arrived, continue to wait on the Lord, knowing that he promises to renew your strength and mount you up like an eagle. If you believe it's your season, then push! The world needs to see what you have been carrying and the Kingdom of God awaits the impact from your delivery.

Prayer – Father, I thank you that you are not slack concerning your promises. I pray that you will teach me how to wait until my season for birthing arrives. Help me not to push prematurely because I want what you placed in me to be fully developed so that the Kingdom of God can be impacted, and you get the glory. In Jesus' name, amen.

What Season Am I in?

"But they who wait for the Lord shall renew their strength; they shall mount up with wings like eagles; they shall run and not be weary; they shall walk and not faint."- (Isaiah 40:31, ESE)

What is God telling me today?

What am I praying for today?

A Heart of Gratitude

"I will praise God's name in song and glorify him with thanksgiving." – Psalm 69:30 (NIV)

Today I am thankful for:

SEASON OF BREAKTHROUGH (PEREZ)

"So David went to Baal Perazim, and there he defeated them. He said, 'As waters break out, the Lord has broken out against my enemies before me.' So that place was called Baal Perazim." - (2 Sam. 5:20, NIV)

God called David "A man after His own heart". He understood what it felt like to break through situations that did not look like the promise he was given. David defeated the enemy. He saw fit to call the place Baal Perazim because it represented the place where the God of breakthrough came through for his people.

Have you ever been there, where your promise did not match your present condition? Where you are looking at the situation and asking how can this be? This is not what God promised!

Tamar, Judah's daughter-in-law, became pregnant by him and gave birth to twins by the name of Perez and Zerah. Perez's name means to bring forth, breakthrough. When his brother, Zerah, pulled his hand back into the womb from being tagged first, Perez pushed his way through and broke out of her womb first. We serve the God of the breakthrough. The God that will allow you to push past what may be holding you back and allow you to break out. We serve a God

He will shift your season so your breakthrough can come when no one expects it to. He wants you to know that your breakthrough is closer than you think.

If you are feeling like God has forgotten you, He has not! He is a promise keeper. Isaiah 46:9-11(NLT) states "Remember the things I have done in the past. For I alone am God! I am God, and there is none like me. Only I can tell you the future before it even happens. Everything I plan will come to pass, for I do whatever I wish. I will call a swift bird of prey from the east; a leader from a distant land to come and do my bidding. I have said what I would do, and I will do it." Can you see your promise in the spirit realm? Do you believe that God is a promise keeper? Do you trust His Word? If so, begin to declare that this is your season of breakthrough. God is calling you to break out of your comfort zone; push past your limitations and begin to walk into what He has called you to walk into. He has already declared your ending from your beginning. Push open the doors of opportunity and grab a hold of what is yours. He is a God that cannot lie. If He said it, take Him at His word and watch Him work.

Prayer – Lord, thank you for being the God of the breakthrough. Thank you for giving me the strength to break through and break out of what has been holding me back. Lord teach me never to give up and how to give you thanks even while I am waiting for my breakthrough. In Jesus' name, amen.

Reflection

Season of Breakthrough and Breakout

"So David went to Baal Perazim, and there he defeated them. He said, 'As waters break out, the Lord has broken out against my enemies before me.' So that place was called Baal Perazim." - (2 Sam. 5:20, NIV)

What is God telling me today?

What am I praying for today?

A Heart of Gratitude

"I will give you thanks in the great assembly; among the throngs I will praise you." – Psalm 35:18 (NIV)

Today I am thankful for:

THE PROMISE KEEPER

"For you have need of patient endurance [to bear up under difficult circumstances without compromising], so that when you have carried out the will of God, you may receive and enjoy to the full what is promised." (Heb. 10:36, AMP)

Genesis chapter 38 gives the account of Judah's second born son Onan. His name meant strength and power. After the death of his brother Er, he was instructed by his father to become the husband of his brother's widow so that she may bear sons to continue the bloodline through which Jesus would eventually come. Onan was willing to enjoy the pleasure of laying with Tamar, but not willing to bear the burden of caring for or raising sons that would not be credited to him. Onan decided to waste his seed and his selfishness caused his death.

Has God appointed you or someone in your life to become a carrier of a promise? Leah's hand maiden was willing to carry sons on her behalf to keep the promise of God moving forward. God may have appointed someone to carry something for you and they refused. That does not mean that what God has promised is dead. It may just mean that He's willing to use another vessel to carry out His mandate. Your promise may be delayed, but it is not denied. Maybe

God has appointed you to be the carrier for someone. Are you willing to go the extra mile so that God's promise may be revealed? God is not slack concerning His promises. Whatever He said, that will He do. If the person that is assigned to you just wants the pleasure without the pain, then continue to patiently endure without compromising because the God who is faithful promises that you will receive the reward if you are willing to endure to the end. Being delayed does not mean that you are denied. Continue to trust in the Promise Keeper to bring forth His promises in your life.

Onan wasted the seed that would ultimately birth the promise because he did not understand the weight of what he was carrying. Make sure you understand the weight of the anointing on your life and not just want to enjoy the pleasure of carrying the anointing, but also the pain that goes along with doing so.

Who is God commissioning you to carry in this season? Make sure you are faithful in doing so.

Prayer – Father, thank you for being a Promise Keeper. I pray that those who are commissioned with the task to be a carrier on my behalf will do so faithfully. Help me to be faithful to carry whatever you commissioned me to carry and for whomever I must carry it. I thank you in advance. In Jesus' name, amen.

The Promise Keeper

"For you have need of patient endurance [to bear up under difficult circumstances without compromising], so that when you have carried out the will of God, you may receive and enjoy to the full what is promised."- (Heb. 10:36, AMP)

What is God telling me today?

What am I praying for today?

A Heart of Gratitude

"I will give thanks to you, Lord, with all my heart; I will tell of all your wonderful deeds." – Psalm 9:1(NIV)

Today I am thankful for:

SEASON OF PETITION (SHELAH)

"Do not be anxious about anything, but in every situation, by prayer and petition, with thanksgiving, present your requests to God. And the peace of God, which transcends all understanding, will guard your hearts and your minds in Christ Jesus." - (Phil. 4: 6-7, NIV)

The third son that was born to Judah was called Shelah. His name meant "petition". Philippians 4: 6-7 tells us to be anxious for nothing. Being anxious according to the dictionary, means that someone is experiencing worry, uneasiness or nervousness about an event or something with an uncertain outcome. The verse also tells us to petition God with thanksgiving and let Him know our request. If we are given such a guarantee, why are we worried? Worrying never solves any situation. As much as Leah knew that she was unloved by Jacob, she did not have the ability to change the situation, but she had the ability to change the outcome of her reaction to the situation. Leah petitioned God but for the wrong reasons. She was petitioning God to let Jacob love her. It is ok to petition to fulfill our desires, however; does the situation that I am petitioning God for line up with the promises and the Word of God? Are we willing to thank and praise Him even if the answer we received does not line up with our petition?

Leah attached her petition to her situation. Let him see me; let him know me more and let him love me. She was petitioning God to let Jacob love her and at the time he did not have the capacity to do so. God wanted Leah to petition Him to show her how to love Him more and praise Him amid a situation that was not the most comfortable. What are you petitioning God for today or in this season? Is it in alignment with the Word of God? As you petition God for what you want, are you doing what Psalm 37 instructed you to do — Delight yourself in the Lord; and He will give you the desires of your heart? If not, begin to delight yourself in Him and watch Him move on your behalf.

Prayer – Father, I thank you that you are a God that cannot lie. A God that does not go back on his word. Whatever your word says, that you promise to do. Holy Spirit, teach me how to petition the Father so that I am in alignment with the Word. Teach me how to petition you not just based on my situation but also on my praise. In Jesus' name, amen.

My Season of Petition

"Do not be anxious about anything, but in every situation, by prayer and petition, with thanksgiving, present your requests to God. And the peace of God, which transcends all understanding, will guard your hearts and your minds in Christ Jesus." - (Phil. 4: 6-7, NIV)

What is God telling me today?

____

____

____

____

____

____

____

What am I praying for today?

____

____

____

____

____

____

____

____

A Heart of Gratitude

"Oh give thanks to the Lord, for he is good, for his steadfast love endures forever!" – Psalm 107:1(ESV)

Today I am thankful for:

SEASON OF RISING UP (ZERAH)

"Do not rejoice over me, O my enemy. Though I fall I will rise; Though I dwell in darkness, the Lord is a light for me." - (Micah 7:8, KJV)

Zerah was the second born but was really meant to be the first-born son of Tamar, Jacob's daughter-in-law who became pregnant by him. During her labor, he pushed forth his arm to indicate being the first; however, his brother Perez pushed his way past him and was born first. When he pushed his arm out, the midwife tied a scarlet thread around his wrist to indicate that he was the first. His name meant "rising up". It also signifies sun, the joy of life and love.

The scarlet thread that was placed around his wrist did not get forgotten even though he was pushed out of the way. It was there as a reminder that he was destined to be first. He was destined to have his name in the history books.

Are you in a season where you are feeling forgotten because it seems like you are not first in line for what you are desiring? Have you fallen and it seems like you have not been able to get back up? Don't forget what your name means! Don't forget that according to Micah 7:8, God has already declared that your enemy should not rejoice over you because though you fall, He will allow you to rise because He is a light for you.

Even though in this season it seems like your enemy is getting ahead of you, continue to hold your head up. Even though your situation does not match what your name indicates, trust God to see you through. You will rise and walk according to what God has birthed out in the earth realm to accomplish. Rise up and let the enemy know like Job that though you are slain, yet you will continue to trust God because He is the God that never goes back on his word. Even though you may be second in line, God will allow others to be skipped over like he did for Judah and allow the blessings to fall on you.

Isaiah 43:19 (KJV) declares, "Behold, I am doing a new thing; now it springs forth, do you not perceive it? I will make a way in the wilderness and rivers in the desert". Just Trust God!

Prayer – Father, I thank you for this season in my life. Thank you that even when I did not feel like I was in a place of rising you reminded me that you will cause me to rise above the enemy. Thank you that I can declare that I am the head and not the tail, above and not beneath because I will rise above my circumstances and give you praise. In Jesus' name, amen!

Season of Rising Up

"Do not rejoice over me, O my enemy. Though I fall I will rise; Though dwell in darkness, the Lord is a light for me." - (Micah 7:8, KJV)

What is God telling me today?

____

____

____

____

____

____

____

What am I praying for today?

____

____

____

____

____

____

____

____

A Heart of Gratitude

"Now, our God, we give you thanks, and praise your glorious name." –1 Chronicles 29:13 (NIV)

Today I am thankful for:

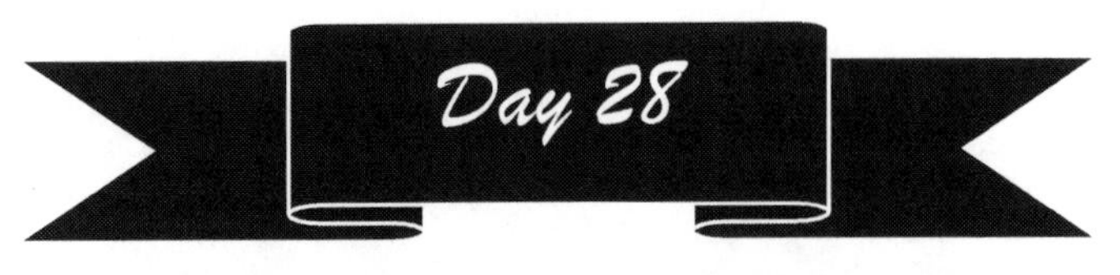

MY LATENT SEASON

"Who hath heard such a thing? Who hath seen such things? Shall the earth be made to bring forth in one day? Or shall a nation be born at once? For as soon as Zion travailed, she brought forth her children." - (Isaiah 66:8, KJV)

When I was giving birth to my daughter, the nurse placed a device on my belly to monitor when contractions were coming and how far apart they were. The action they took was based on what was happening on the monitor. During the latent stage, the woman's cervix is beginning to open in preparation for the baby to be born. God is ready to move based on your actions.

The children of Israel were in bondage, they were in great anguish and desperately wanted God to deliver them. Amid their desperation, they cried out to God, and He heard and delivered them.

In your latent season it may feel like you are enduring pain that you have not felt before, you may be feeling desperate and forgotten, but God has not forgotten you. He sees your travailing and is just preparing you for the beginning of a great season. God is beginning to open your spiritual womb and even though He is doing that, the pain may be irregular and some may last longer than others; continue

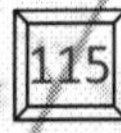

to travail for the manifestation to come forth. Trust Him in the process. Sometimes it may hurt, other times it may feel like now is the appointed time. Psalm 27:4 says, "Wait on the Lord: be of good courage, and He shall strengthen thine heart: wait, I say, on the Lord".

Amid your travailing God has your back! He is preparing you for a great season of your life. In the latent stage the woman's womb tightens and then relaxes. God is saying when you feel the pressure the most, He has your back, and you can just relax in Him because He promises never to leave or forsake you. The spiritual pain that you are feeling is just a sign of what to come. Continue to press into God. Continue to travail; continue to believe God for what He is doing in your life in this season.

Prayer – Lord, I thank you for being with me in my seasons of pain. In my season when I seem like I have no one to turn to and my pain is getting sharper, you send your Word to comfort and guide me. You send your Holy Spirit to direct my every step as You wrap your loving arms around me. Thank you, Lord. In Jesus' name, amen.

The Latent Season

"Who hath heard such a thing? Who hath seen such things? Shall the earth be made to bring forth in one day? Or shall a nation be born at once? For as soon as Zion travailed, she brought forth her children." – (Isaiah 66:8, KJV)

What is God telling me today?

____

____

____

____

____

____

____

What am I praying for today?

____

____

____

____

____

____

____

____

A Heart of Gratitude

"I will give thanks to the Lord because of his righteousness; I will sing the praises of the name of the Lord Most High." – Psalm 7:17(NIV)

Today I am thankful for:

MY ACTIVE SEASON

"For I consider that the sufferings of this present time are not worth comparing with the glory that is to be revealed to us." - (Rom. 8:18, ESE)

As I endured the pain of contractions and at times became tired, I understood that what was getting ready to come forth would have been worth the pain. What I patiently waited on for almost 40 weeks was about to be manifested. The nurses in my room were giving me instructions on what to do and when to do it.

You have endured the trials and temptation. You have endured the pain. You did not allow what you went through to prevent you from getting to this season in your life. Right now, as in the natural, you may be feeling the cramps that come along with this season; you may even want to give up because the pain is getting intense, but I want to encourage you to hold on. Psalm 30: 5b tells us "Weeping may endure for a night, but joy is coming in the morning." What you are experiencing in this season cannot be compared to what God is getting ready to reveal. You cannot give up now. Galatians 6:9 says "Let us not grow weary or become discouraged in doing good, for at the proper time we will reap, if we do not give in". Just as the nurses were there to guide me, the Holy Spirit is guiding you through this season. Your reaping moment is closer than you think. Keep pushing, your season of manifestation is close at hand.

As the pain becomes more intense, the discomfort may become too much to handle. The doctor may give the patient some medication to ease the pain; the mother may have to get someone to give them a massage; she may even have to take a warm bath, or she may just have to change and reposition herself for what is happening. In this season, I declare that a shifting is taking place as you reposition yourself for a fresh revelation of what God is doing. I pray for the Holy Spirit to ease your pain as you meditate upon Him through prayer and worship. Allow Him to permeate your whole being and bring you the comfort you are needing to press forward. You are pressing towards the mark and the pressing did not come to break you, but to make you.

Prayer – Father, I thank you for being a present help in my times of trouble. I pray that as I press towards the higher calling I will remain focused. I declare that I will not grow weary because I will reap if I do not faint. I thank you that even though at times I did not feel you, I knew you were still there. When I was overwhelmed and it seemed like my situation would have the best of me, you sent your Holy Spirit to comfort me and for that I say thank you. In Jesus name, amen.

Reflection

<u>My Active Season</u>

"For I consider that the sufferings of this present time are not worth comparing with the glory that is to be revealed to us."- (Rom. 8:18, ESE)

What is God telling me today?

What am I praying for today?

A Heart of Gratitude

"I will give thanks to the Lord because of his righteousness; I will sing the praises of the name of the Lord Most High." – Psalm 7:17 (NIV)

Today I am thankful for:

MY TRANSITIONAL SEASON

"I have been crucified with Christ. It is no longer I who live, but Christ who lives in me. And the life I now live in the flesh I live by faith in the Son of God, who loved me and gave himself for me." - (Gal. 2:20, ESV)

While giving birth to my son, another patient was giving birth to twins and the anesthesiologist had to be in the room with the attending doctor. He was not able to get to me and I was fully dilated and ready to give birth. The pain was so intense that during my labor, I told my doctor I was not going to push until I received something to help with the pain. My doctor told me that I was too far along to get any pain medication and I just needed to push. The contractions were closer, and I was beginning to feel pressure all over. Even though the contractions were intense, I still had to wait on the nurse or doctor to tell me when to push. If I pushed too soon it would make me tired and may even cause a delay in the delivery.

Pressure is a sign of transformation taking place. Butterflies must endure the process to show forth its beauty; grapes must be crushed; diamonds can only be formed under pressure; olives must be pressed. Any seed that springs forth from the ground normally begins their process in the darkness of being buried. You are feeling like you're in the dark being crushed, under pressure and being pressed because you are in your transitional season.

What are you feeling in this season? Is your pain getting more intense? Are you feeling uncomfortable in your present position? Are you feeling the urge to push? I want to encourage you to be still and listen to the voice of the Holy Spirit in this season. What is He telling you to do? It's pushing time! Philippians 1:6 states, "I am convinced and confident of this very thing, that He who has begun a good work in you will [continue to] perfect and complete it until the day of Christ Jesus [the time of His return]." He started the work, and He will continue to perfect that which He has placed in you to be manifested. He has brought you to your transitional season!

You have allowed the seed of His Word to be planted into your spirit; you have labored in prayer and in His Word, you have spent time in His Presence and have pressed your ear against His mouth to hear what He is saying. You have shifted, repositioned and allowed yourself to go from not just hearing His voice, but to listening to what He is saying, and you acted on His Word. This is your season of transition. This is your season to evolve into the butterfly He has destined you to become. This is your season that He has moved you from enough to more than enough. This is your season where the dust that was blinding you during your hardest time has settled and God has allowed you to stand when everything around you was crumbling.

This is your rewarding season because you endured as a good soldier. This is the season according to Psalm 47:10 where you became still to recognize and acknowledge that indeed He is the God who has carried you through to this season.

Prayer – Father, I acknowledge that you are King of Kings and Lord of Lords. I acknowledge you as the Omnipotent, Omniscient, Omnipresent God. The God who is the all-knowing and the all wise God. To you be glory, dominion, majesty, and power. Thank you for being the Lord over my life. Thank you for allowing me not to collapse under the pressure. Not to give up when I felt like it. Not to listen to the noise around me, but to press on toward the mark for the prize of your higher calling. In Jesus' name, amen.

My Transitional Season

"I have been crucified with Christ. It is no longer I who live, but Christ who lives in me. And the life I now live in the flesh I live by faith in the Son of God, who loved me and gave himself for me." - (Gal. 2:20, ESV)

What is God telling me today?

____

____

____

____

____

____

____

What am I praying for today?

____

____

____

____

____

____

____

____

A Heart of Gratitude

"Let us come before him with thanksgiving and extol him with music and song. For the Lord is the great God the great King above all gods." – Psalm 95:2-3 (NIV)

Today I am thankful for:

Acknowledgement

I want to thank God for the guidance of the Holy Spirit throughout my writing process. I am thankful to my sisters who believed in what I was being directed to do and pushed me every step of the way to complete what God started in me. I am so thankful for a mother who always has my back! She always believed in me and encouraged me to go all the way.

To my husband of 29 years, Pastor David Stewart and my two children, Davena and David Jr., thank you! You have been my rock and I am so thankful and grateful that I was chosen to be married to such an awesome man of God and the carrier of two children that were birthed out to be world changers.

To all those that had a part in my journey, and pushed me when I did not feel like it. Stayed up just to check over what I was writing, and called to make sure I was staying focused, thank you.

Forward

For over 15 years I have had the privilege of being mentored, pastored, mothered, and groomed into the woman I am today by Pastor Desrene Stewart. Pastor Desrene has made a remarkable impact in every area of my life. She taught me the true essence of a worshipper, the value of being a Proverbs 31 wife, the essences of being an entrepreneur, and most importantly how to be a fulfilled woman. As a worshipper, she has led thousands of us to the feet of Jesus through her unique gift of tapping into the presence of God effortlessly. I have served under her ministry for many years, while learning the principles of being a multi-faceted Kingdom woman. Little did I know that I was planting seeds of service, as I now stand as a Pastor, Mother, Mentor and Entrepreneur. The keys to Pastor Desrene's far reaching, sustainable Kingdom impact is her refined grace and humility. She knows who she is, what her purpose is and commands her respect without devaluing others. She stands tall with such ownership of her gift and makes no room for compromise. She understands her Kingdom's purpose and executes it on and off the stage.

Birthing Praise out of Pain is a book that has been lived by Pastor Desrene. The principles found in this book have been fortified with many years of ministry and personal experiences, transcending race, gender, age, and socio-economic status. The wealth of truths found in this book will break down mental, emotional, and spiritual barriers that have plagued many for years.

This is not just another book, this is a spiritual plan for God's people.

In this era of unprecedented chaos, unpredictability, loss and pain, Pastor Desrene is releasing an on time, Kingdom mandate that will cause many people to be set free. Regardless of where we are on our life's journey; we are either experiencing a painful situation, leaving one or about to enter one. It is important we all grab hold of the wisdom from this book. Flipping the script on pain and choosing praise is not easy or natural, especially when that pain cuts deep. But Pastor Desrene is offering us an alternative. Choosing to praise our way through the pain is possible through Christ Jesus. You are not alone, Pastor Desrene and I have come to realize that pain is not the end of our stories. We have an alternative! Praising our way through fears, anxieties, and stress allows us to focus on the power of our praise. We have a weapon to combat pain, it's our PRAISE!

May the Lord open your eyes, heart and soul to the healing, deliverance, and peace you will receive by reading this book. I know it will edify your spirit and set you free from the devastation of pain. As you praise, freedom will chase after you, like it did me.

Dr. Cindy Khan-Jordan, Pastor, Ph.D.

The message Birthing Praise Out of Your Pain was conceived and delivered in a season when I didn't quite understand what God was doing, where He was trying to take me or even what He was preparing me to experience.

I decided to walk away from my job of 14 years to start my own business. Little did I know that God had a different plan. God allowed me to enter the most challenging season I've ever been through and travelled on a journey I never thought I would ever go through because I made all the right choices in getting my education and making sure I had all the right tools to be successful.

I had plans to start my own business and when that fell through, and the Holy Spirit spoke this Word to me; "Did you ask what is it that I wanted you to do?" I realized that I did not truly seek God for his directions. That Word took me on a journey where I gained experience and insight that I would never have had if I did not go on the journey. I was preparing for bible study when the Holy Spirit took me into the book of Genesis and helped me to see Leah, Jacob's wife through a new lens. Amid a painful season of her life, she learned how to praise God through her pain. Even though my journey was painful and at times unbearable, it took me into places like Australia, Europe and throughout the USA where I had the opportunity to minister the Word of God and share my testimony of what I was still going through while I was travelling to minster God's Word.

I now look back and firmly believe that God wanted me to not only minister from His Word, but to also have an experience to go with what I was ministering. Birthing Praise Out of Your Pain, has been one of the most powerful messages I have ever delivered. I am grateful for the opportunity to put this life changing message into the form of a daily devotion and pray that the Holy Spirit will use the words to minister into your lives daily and help you to know that even during your most painful and challenging season you can birth out praise.

In His Service,

Pastor Desrene Stewart

Made in United States
Orlando, FL
29 April 2022

17317008R00076